39 DAZZLING EXPERIMENTS WITH DRY ICE

By Brian Rohrig

FizzBang Science

The photos included in the text are not intended to imply a commercial endorsement of any product.

All experiments in this book are to performed only under competent adult supervision. Neither the author nor the publisher assume any liability whatsoever for any damage caused or injury sustained while performing the experiments contained in this book.

FizzBang Science
807 Murlay Drive
Plain City, Ohio 43064
www.fizzbangscience.com
info@fizzbangscience.com

ISBN 0-9718480-3-3

For Miss Betty Lewis,
my high school Chemistry teacher
from 1978 to 1980,
at Ironton High School in
Ironton, Ohio,
who first instilled in me a
love for Chemistry.

ACKNOWLEDGEMENTS

Thanks to Frank Reuter for carefully and thoroughly editing this text. Any and all errors are strictly my own.

Illustrations by Michele Murphy

Books printed by Network Printers in Milwaukee, Wisconsin

Cover design by Kristi Gerner

I would like to thank Robert Becker, chemistry teacher at Kirkwood High School in Kirkwood, Missouri, for graciously granting me permission to include in this book two dry ice experiments he originated: the leaky faucet and the dry ice crystal ball.

The website **www.dryiceinfo.com** contained a wealth of useful information that was invaluable in compling this book.

TABLE OF CONTENTS

INTRODUCTION

I still remember the first time I saw dry ice – that mystical solid white substance that emanated mysterious vapors and disappeared before my eyes, and which was absolutely forbidden to touch. Since then, it has always held a special fascination for me. As a science teacher, I include dry ice in my lesson plans several times each year. One of my students' favorite days of the year is "Dry Ice Day," when we do a series of wonderful experiments with dry ice, culminating in the making of homemade root beer. I have demonstrated these same experiments for all ages, and have invariably found young and old alike to share in my fascination for this amazing substance. Thus came the impetus for writing this book – the third in the "39 Experiments" series.

The goal of each book in this series is to present in easily understandable language unique experiments using readily obtainable substances that will get kids – and adults – excited about science. I sincerely believe that you will thoroughly enjoy each of the 39 experiments presented here. Each has been performed by me and countless others numerous times, so you can rest assured that each experiment can be successfully accomplished with a minimum of effort.

Hopefully this book will give you 39 reasons to go out and purchase some dry ice so you can have some "very cool" fun!

39 Dazzling Experiments with Dry Ice

WHERE CAN I FIND DRY ICE?

Dry Ice can be obtained from numerous sources. The easiest way is to look in the Yellow Pages under "Ice" or "Dry Ice" and call up a local dealer. Most large cities have dealers who sell dry ice for about a dollar per pound, or less if bought in bulk. Or you can sometimes purchase dry ice from convenience and grocery stores. Since frozen foods such as meat and ice cream are often shipped in dry ice, you may even be able to get some free of charge if you find out when deliveries are made. If you live in a college or university town, check with the physics or chemistry department where researchers often make their own.

To find out if dry ice is available in your area, visit the following web site:

http://www.dryicedirectory.com.

Once you are at the site, you will be directed to enter in your telephone area code. You will then receive a list of all suppliers in your area.

HOW DO I STORE DRY ICE?

Depending on the amount, dry ice can last for several days in an ordinary picnic cooler. The best way to store dry ice is to line the cooler with newspapers, put in the dry ice, and then stuff newspapers on top and all around the dry ice. Do not store in an airtight container, since the dry ice will still be undergoing sublimation, with the release of gas, which could cause a container to explode. An ordinary picnic cooler with a lift-off lid will work fine, since the lid is not rigidly attached (as with a latch); the cooler should provide a tight enough fit to prevent appreciable loss of the dry ice. Never store dry ice in a container with a screw-on lid (such as a thermos or an insulated jug) – as the container will most definitely explode due to the buildup of gas!

Never store dry ice in an ordinary freezer, since the moving air currents will cause rapid sublimation. Store your dry ice in a cooler and keep in a still, cool place until you are ready to use it. A basement will work fine, or a garage if it is cool. Do not store in the trunk of your car on a hot day, or you will have little left when it comes time to use it! Always order a little more than you need, since some will sublimate no matter how well you store it.

HOW IS DRY ICE MADE?

If you visit a company that makes their own dry ice, you will notice large tanks filled with liquid carbon dioxide. Carbon dioxide will liquefy at a pressure of 59 atm (atmospheres) or 870 psi (pounds per square inch). This is 59 times greater than normal atmospheric pressure! To make dry ice, an expansion valve is opened on the tank, which releases some of the liquid CO_2. Since the pressure of the CO_2 is drastically reduced, the liquid changes phase, rapidly evaporating into gaseous CO_2. Evaporation is an endothermic process, absorbing energy from its surroundings. (Think about why you sweat – the evaporation of this moisture absorbs heat from your body and keeps you cool.) Due to this rapid evaporation of liquid CO_2, the temperature of the remaining liquid drops rapidly. Once the temperature drops to $-78.5°C$ ($-109.3°F$), the liquid carbon dioxide will freeze into solid dry ice. A hydraulic press is then used to compress this dry ice into a large block, using up to 60 tons of pressure. A 50 lb block can be produced in 60 seconds.

WHAT IS DRY ICE USED FOR?

There are numerous uses for dry ice, as you will soon discover in the following pages. Here are a few commercial uses for dry ice:

- Creating special effects in plays, movies, dances, and other productions (often used in fog machines).
- Shipping frozen foods, such as meat, ice cream, and vegetables.
- Keeping foods frozen during camping or during a power outage.
- Carbonating liquids to make carbonated beverages.
- Shrinking small dents in your car.
- Loosening the adhesive so you can remove old floor tile.
- Eradicating gophers and ants from your yard by placing dry ice in their holes.
- Cooling alcohol during the branding of cattle and horses.
- Removing warts.
- Extinguishing fires.
- Attracting mosquitoes in mosquito traps (mosquitoes are attracted by CO_2).
- Cleaning surfaces (a good alternative to sandblasting).
- Shrink fitting metal bushings, sleeves, and bearings.

SAFETY PRECAUTIONS

Please observe the following safety precautions whenever using dry ice:

1. Do all experiments only under direct adult supervision.
2. Never put dry ice in an airtight container, since the sublimating gas that is released may cause the container to explode.
3. Never touch dry ice with your bare skin, since it may cause frostbite. Always wear heavy insulated gloves when handling dry ice.
4. Do not use in an enclosed area or in a room that is not well-ventilated, since CO_2 gas may build up, causing suffocation.
5. Never inhale vapors from dry ice, since CO_2 gas displaces oxygen and may cause suffocation.
6. Always wear safety goggles when doing any experiment involving dry ice.
7. Always store dry ice, or any other chemicals, out of the reach of children.
8. Always read the label of any chemical thoroughly before using.

Experiment #1:
WHAT IS DRY ICE?

Objective: To discover where dry ice gets its name.

Materials:

- Dry Ice
- Insulated gloves
- Candle
- Hammer

Safety Precautions: Use dry ice only with adult supervision. Never touch dry ice with your bare skin – it may cause frostbite! Use dry ice only outdoors or in a well-ventilated room to prevent buildup of carbon dioxide gas. Do not inhale vapors – inhalation of vapors may cause suffocation, since carbon dioxide displaces oxygen.

Procedure:
1. Place a piece of dry ice on a tabletop. It will shrink in size, until it eventually disappears.
2. Now take two pieces of equal size, and break one in small pieces with a hammer. Note how this affects its rate of disappearance.

3. Bring a lit candle near another piece, and note the effect.
4. Take yet another piece and blow across the top (don't bring your lips too close!) What does this do? Can you think of other ways to hasten the rate of disappearance of the dry ice?

Explanation: "Dry Ice" was originally a trade name for solid carbon dioxide, but over time has become the universally accepted term for this amazing substance. Dry ice is so named because it does not melt like ordinary ice, but bypasses the liquid phase, changing directly from a solid to a gas at normal atmospheric pressure. This process is referred to as sublimation. Since dry ice is solid carbon dioxide, anytime it is brought above its sublimation point (-78.5°C), it vaporizes.

Sublimation involves the escaping of molecules from the surface, much like evaporation. By breaking up the chunks of dry ice and exposing more surface area, you dramatically increase the rate of sublimation. Blowing across a piece of dry ice reduces the air pressure above it, making it easier for the molecules of CO_2 to escape. Heating the dry ice causes the molecules to move faster, increasing their rate of escape.

Mothballs and air fresheners also undergo sublimation. Can you think of any other substances that sublimate? Water will also undergo sublimation if it is below its freezing point. If wet laundry is hung outside to dry, it will first freeze and then eventually dry. Ice cubes placed in the freezer will shrink with time. A snow bank will shrink in size even though it remains below freezing. These are all examples of sublimation.

Experiment #2:

MAKING FOG WITH DRY ICE

Objective: To create amazing special effects using fog created with dry ice.

Materials:
- Dry Ice
- Insulated gloves
- Plastic cups
- Hot and cold water
- Aluminum pie pan

Safety Precautions: Use dry ice only with adult supervision. Never touch dry ice with your bare skin – it may cause frostbite! Use dry ice only outdoors or in a well-ventilated room to prevent buildup of carbon dioxide gas. Do not inhale vapors – inhalation of vapors may cause suffocation, since carbon dioxide displaces oxygen.

Procedure:
1. Place a chunk of dry ice in a cup of water from the tap. It will immediately sink to the bottom, bubble vigorously, and produce a thick cloud of fog that will eerily

spread over the top of the cup and then sink downwards.

2. Now place some hot water in another cup and add a chunk of dry ice. What happens?
3. Place an aluminum pie pan over the fog. What do you observe?

Explanation: The white fog that is formed when dry ice is placed in water is commonly used to produce special effects in movies. It is also used at Halloween to produce spooky effects. Even though carbon dioxide is present within the fog, you cannot see it, since CO_2 is always invisible. What you are actually observing are tiny droplets of liquid water that have been dragged up from the water by the carbon dioxide gas that is rapidly sublimating from the submerged piece of dry ice. These tiny water droplets form a visible cloud above the surface of the water. This cloud will cause drops of water to form on the aluminum pie pan. Since this fog is saturated with carbon dioxide, which is denser than air, it hovers very low over the mouth of the cup and then falls downward at the sides.

Experiment # 3:
THE SQUEALING COIN

Objective: To produce amazing sound effects when a coin or spoon is placed on top of a block of dry ice.

Materials:

- Dry Ice
- Insulated gloves
- Coin
- Spoon

Safety Precautions: Use dry ice only with adult supervision. Never touch dry ice with your bare skin – it may cause frostbite! Use dry ice only outdoors or in a well-ventilated room to prevent buildup of carbon dioxide gas. Do not inhale vapors – inhalation of vapors may cause suffocation, since carbon dioxide displaces oxygen.

Procedure:

1. Place a flat block of dry ice on a tabletop. Place a coin on top of the block and observe what happens.
2. Remove the coin and place the convex side of a spoon on the block of dry ice. Apply a little pressure with the spoon. You should

notice a loud squealing sound in both cases.

3. Try other metal objects. Do they produce a similar sound?
4. Try a non-metallic object. What happens?

Explanation: Since dry ice is sublimating so rapidly at room temperature, a constant stream of carbon dioxide gas is being released from its surface. When a coin or spoon is placed on top of a block of dry ice, the gas is being temporarily hindered from escaping. The loud squealing sound is due to the escaping carbon dioxide gas from underneath the object. When pressure is applied with the spoon, pressure builds up as the gas attempts to escape, producing a louder sound.

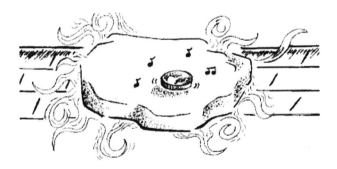

Metals are excellent conductors of heat, and since the metal is initially warmer than the dry ice, heat will be transferred from the metal to the dry ice. This will serve to increase the rate of sublimation. Once the metal cools down after being in contact with the dry ice, the rate of sublimation becomes less, causing the squealing sound to be more subdued. A non-metallic object generally does not produce a sound when placed on dry ice, because non-metals tend to be insulators, which are poor conductors of heat, and therefore have little effect on the sublimation rate of dry ice.

Experiment # 4:
A FILM CANISTER ROCKET

Objective: To demonstrate the principles by which rockets are launched.

Materials:

- Dry Ice
- Insulated gloves
- Transparent film canister with lid that closes tightly
- Water

Safety Precautions:

Wear safety goggles. Never aim or point your rocket at anyone, and step back before launching your rocket. Use dry ice only under adult supervision. Never touch dry ice with your bare skin – it may cause frostbite! Use dry ice only outdoors or in a well-ventilated room to prevent buildup of carbon dioxide gas. Do not inhale vapors – inhalation of vapors may cause suffocation, since carbon dioxide displaces oxygen.

Procedure:

1. Fill the film canister nearly to the top with

water. Drop in a pea-size piece of dry ice, place the lid on tightly, and then step back. The lid will be shot up into the air several feet with a loud popping sound.

2. Try varying the amount of water to see how this affects your results.

3. Try varying the temperature of the water.

4. To truly simulate a rocket, try this experiment with the lid facing downward. The entire body of the film canister will then be launched into the air.

Explanation: This experiment is often performed with an Alka-Seltzer tablet (which releases CO_2 gas upon contact with water), but dry ice is much more effective! As the dry ice sublimates and turns to carbon dioxide vapor, a tremendous amount of pressure builds up within the film canister, causing the lid to be forcibly expelled. When the canister is inverted, the force of the water and gas being expelled downward forces the canister upward.

This experiment verifies Newton's Third Law of Motion, which states that anytime a force is exerted in one direction, an equal force is exerted in the opposite direction. This is the principle under which rockets operate. The force of expanding gases exerted downward as a result of the combustion of rocket fuel causes an equal and opposite force which propels the rocket upward.

Experiment # 5:
MAKING A FOUNTAIN OF SOAP SUDS

Objective: To create a fabulous fountain of soap suds using dry ice.

Materials:

- Dry Ice
- Insulated gloves
- 2-Liter bottle
- Liquid dishwashing soap

Safety Precautions: Use dry ice only with adult supervision. Never touch dry ice with your bare skin – it may cause frostbite! Use dry ice only outdoors or in a well-ventilated room to prevent buildup of carbon dioxide gas. Do not inhale vapors – inhalation of vapors may cause suffocation, since carbon dioxide displaces oxygen.

Procedure:

1. Do this experiment outdoors or in a large sink, since it will make quite a mess. Fill a 2-Liter bottle about halfway with warm water. Squirt in a copious amount of dishwashing liquid.
2. Drop in a chunk of dry ice. Do NOT place

the cap back on the bottle. Stand back and observe an amazing profusion of suds! When the flow of suds decreases, you may add more dry ice.

3. For a variation on the above, place the piece of dry ice in a cup half-filled with just dishwashing liquid with no added water. Will bubbles still form? Try it to find out.

Explanation: Soap suds are an example of a colloid – a liquid with a gas dispersed within it. In this case, the sublimating dry ice produces CO_2 gas, which becomes suspended within the soap-water solution, forming bubbles. When you blow bubbles, you are introducing air into a bubble solution. In this case, however, the gas is carbon dioxide, which forms a profusion of bubbles as the dry ice sublimates. By increasing the temperature of the water, the bubbles can be made to form more quickly.

39 Dazzling Experiments with Dry Ice

Experiment # 6:

MAKING A FIRE EXTINGUISHER

Objective: To discover the fire-fighting abilities of carbon dioxide.

Materials:

- Dry Ice
- Insulated gloves
- Cup
- Candle and matches
- Wooden coffee stirrer

Safety Precautions: Use dry ice only with adult supervision. Never touch dry ice with your bare skin – it may cause frostbite! Use dry ice only outdoors or in a well-ventilated room to prevent buildup of carbon dioxide gas. Do not inhale vapors – inhalation of vapors may cause suffocation, since carbon dioxide displaces oxygen. Keep matches away from any combustible materials.

Procedure:

1. Place a piece of dry ice in a cup of water and observe the rapid sublimation leading to the formation of a cloud.

2. Light a wooden coffee stirrer and bring it near the cloud. It will immediately be extinguished.
3. Next, light a candle, and attempt to extinguish the candle by pouring the CO_2 gas over the flame. Be careful not to pour any of the water from the cup, but pour only the fog, which is saturated with CO_2 gas.

Explanation: Dry ice that is undergoing sublimation makes an excellent fire extinguisher due to the presence of carbon dioxide gas. Carbon dioxide essentially displaces the oxygen in the air, making the fire go out. The same thing can be observed when a lit match is placed within the mouth of a freshly opened bottle of soda. The flame will be extinguished due to the release of carbon dioxide gas that exists in the space above the liquid.

CO_2 gas can be poured because it is denser than air. Many fire extinguishers today rely on carbon dioxide gas. They also leave no mess, just like dry ice. If you observe a fire extinguisher as it is being discharged, you will actually see little flecks of dry ice immediately forming. This is due to the extreme temperature drop resulting from the drastic reduction in pressure that accompanies the carbon dioxide as it is released from the fire extinguisher. The formation of dry ice proves that the CO_2 is actually below -78.5°C as it leaves the nozzle of the extinguisher. This low temperature makes the CO_2 extinguisher especially effective, since it also serves to bring substances far below their kindling temperature. The kindling temperature is the minimum temperature required for a substance to burn.

Experiment # 7:
A HEAVY BALLOON

Objective: To demonstrate that carbon dioxide is denser than air.

Materials:

- Dry Ice
- Insulated gloves
- 20 oz plastic soda bottle
- Balloons

Safety Precautions: Use dry ice only with adult supervision. Never touch dry ice with your bare skin – it may cause frostbite! Use dry ice only outdoors or in a well-ventilated room to prevent buildup of carbon dioxide gas. Do not inhale vapors – inhalation of vapors may cause suffocation, since carbon dioxide displaces oxygen.

Procedure:

1. Fill a 20 oz plastic soda bottle about halfway with water and then add a piece of dry ice. Under no circumstances should the bottle be capped.
2. Fit a balloon over the mouth of the bottle, extending it past the threads. After the balloon has expanded, carefully remove it

and then tie it off.
3. Drop the balloon to the ground and note its rate of fall.
4. Now inflate another balloon by blowing it up with normal air to the same size as the carbon dioxide-filled balloon. Drop it and the carbon dioxide-filled balloon to the ground at the same time. What do you observe?

Explanation: A balloon filled with carbon dioxide will fall faster than a balloon filled with just air, since carbon dioxide is denser than air. Although gravity accelerates all objects downward at the same rate, the buoyant force of the air acting upward will have a greater effect on the lighter balloon. Thus, heavier objects will tend to fall a little faster than very light objects if both have the same volume. Consider a helium balloon. It rises because the buoyant force of the air pushing up on it is greater than the weight of the balloon, which is indeed very small.

Experiment # 8:
FLOATING BUBBLES

Objective: To demonstrate that air-filled bubbles will float on a layer of carbon dioxide.

Materials:

- Dry Ice
- Insulated gloves
- Bottle of commercial bubble solution with bubble blower
- 10-gallon aquarium or equivalent

Safety Precautions: Use dry ice only with adult supervision. Never touch dry ice with your bare skin – it may cause frostbite! Use dry ice only outdoors or in a well-ventilated room to prevent buildup of carbon dioxide gas. Do not inhale vapors – inhalation of vapors may cause suffocation, since carbon dioxide displaces oxygen.

Procedure:

1. Place a large piece of dry ice in an aquarium and cover with a board or piece of sturdy cardboard.
2. After a half-hour or so, remove the cover and blow some bubbles down into the

aquarium. What happens?

3. Come back and try to repeat this experiment an hour or so later. Is the carbon dioxide still there? Is it necessary to even keep the aquarium covered?

Explanation: The bubbles will very noticeably float on the layer of carbon dioxide gas that has formed on the bottom of the aquarium. It will be very difficult to get a bubble to remain on the bottom of the aquarium as long as carbon dioxide is present. This experiment demonstrates again that carbon dioxide is denser than air. Much of the carbon dioxide formed from the sublimating dry ice will remain at the bottom of the aquarium. This carbon dioxide is clearly denser than the air-filled bubbles, causing them to float on an invisible layer of heavy gas.

Experiment # 9:
COLOSSAL COLOR CHANGES

Objective: To discover if adding dry ice to water will change the pH of the resulting solution.

Materials:
- Dry Ice
- Insulated gloves
- Water
- Plastic cups or 2-Liter bottles
- Bromothymol blue indicator solution (available from a pet shop or pool supply store)
- Magic Ink (available from a magic store or hobby shop)
- Red cabbage
- Ammonia
- Eyedropper

Safety Precautions:
Acid/base indicators are poisonous – store out of reach of children. Ammonia is also poisonous – do not inhale vapors. Use dry ice only with adult supervision. Never touch dry ice with your bare skin – it may cause frostbite! Use dry ice only outdoors or in a well-ventilated room to prevent buildup of carbon dioxide gas. Do not inhale

vapors – inhalation of vapors may cause suffocation, since carbon dioxide displaces oxygen.

Procedure:

1. Pour enough water into a transparent cup, bottle, or cylinder so that it is 3/4 full.
2. Add enough bromothymol blue to turn the color a deep blue.
3. Now add a few chunks of dry ice and observe. The color will change from blue to green and finally to yellow!
4. To reverse the process, add just enough ammonia with an eyedropper to change the color back to blue. Adding dry ice will change the color back to yellow. This same cycle can be repeated numerous times.
5. For a variation, add some Magic Ink to water. Dry ice will change it from deep blue to colorless.
6. Boil some red cabbage leaves in some water in a pan on the stove. The water will turn a deep bluish purple color. This will be your red cabbage solution. Add this to a cylinder of water until the water is a deep bluish purple color.
7. Now add just enough ammonia with an eyedropper to turn the water green. When the dry ice is added, it will turn from green to blue to red, with a variety of intermediate hues.

Explanation: Adding dry ice to water forms a solution of carbonic acid. The reaction is as follows:

$$CO_{2(g)} + H_2O_{(l)} \Rightarrow H_2CO_{3(aq)}$$

The purpose of adding the bromothymol blue is to indicate the presence of an acid. Acids will turn an aqueous solution containing bromothymol blue first green and then yellow. This indicates a lowering of the pH, which is a measure of how acidic (or basic) a substance is. If we assume tap water to be neutral (having a pH of 7), adding dry ice will generally lower the pH to around 5 or 6. Adding ammonia, which is basic, will neutralize the carbonic acid and raise the pH, causing the bromothymol blue solution to turn blue again.

Magic ink contains thymolphthalein, which is deep blue in a basic solution and colorless in an acid. When squirted on a white shirt, it relies on CO_2 in the air to turn it colorless. Dry ice has the same effect.

Red cabbage contains a pigment known as anthocyanin, which functions as an acid/base indicator. It turns green in the presence of a base and red in the presence of an acid.

Many other acid/base indicators will produce this same effect. Ask your local high school chemistry teacher or look in a chemical supply catalogue for additional indicators that will change a variety of colors when dry ice is added to an aqueous solution containing this indicator. Some interesting ones to try are universal indicator, phenolphthalein, and phenol red.

BLUE ⇄ GREEN ⇄ YELLOW

Experiment # 10:
BUBBLE ART

Objective: To paint beautiful images of bubbles using dry ice.

Materials:

- Dry Ice
- Insulated gloves
- Tempera paint (available from an art or office supply store)
- Cups
- White cardboard or large index cards
- Dish detergent

Safety Precautions: Use dry ice only with adult supervision. Never touch dry ice with your bare skin – it may cause frostbite! Use dry ice only outdoors or in a well-ventilated room to prevent buildup of carbon dioxide gas. Do not inhale vapors – inhalation of vapors may cause suffocation, since carbon dioxide displaces oxygen.

Procedure:

1. Add two teaspoonfuls of Tempera paint to a cup of water and stir well.
2. Squirt some dishwashing liquid into the cup. Add a chunk of dry ice to the cup.

This will cause the paint solution to bubble. Place a piece of white cardboard or a large index card on top of the cup.

3. Remove the card. You will see beautiful painted images of bubbles on the card. You will need to experiment with your technique in order to perfect the method that forms the best bubbles.

Explanation: As the dry ice sublimes, it forms carbon dioxide gas. This gas mixes with the paint and soap solution to form colored bubbles. When these colored bubbles come into contact with the cardboard, their image is left behind.

Experiment # 11:
AIR HOCKEY

Objective: To play "air hockey" using dry ice.

Materials:

- Dry Ice
- Insulated gloves
- Long tabletop

Safety Precautions: Use dry ice only with adult supervision. Never touch dry ice with your bare skin – it may cause frostbite! Use dry ice only outdoors or in a well-ventilated room to prevent buildup of carbon dioxide gas. Do not inhale vapors – inhalation of vapors may cause suffocation, since carbon dioxide displaces oxygen.

Procedure:

Make sure you wear insulated gloves at all times during this activity. Station two people at opposite ends of a long table and gently push a chunk of dry ice back and forth. The piece of dry ice will act like a puck and each of your gloved hands can represent a hockey stick. You can make the experiment into a game and devise your own rules for playing and scoring. What you will notice is that the piece of dry ice will glide effortlessly across the tabletop, requiring very little force.

Explanation: An actual air hockey game operates due to reduced friction. This is due to a layer of air over the top of the playing surface that makes movement of a small puck across the surface nearly effortless. The dry ice glides effortlessly for this same reason, except that the lack of friction is due to a layer of carbon dioxide gas that is being released by the sublimating dry ice. The chunk of dry ice glides very easily along this layer of CO_2, reducing the friction between the piece of ice and the tabletop. It is this lack of friction that makes driving or walking on ice so difficult. If there was a complete lack of friction and a hockey rink was of infinite size, a hockey puck once started in motion would never stop! This verifies Newton's First Law of Motion, which states that an object will continue in motion in a straight line unless some force acts to stop it.

Experiment # 12:
STUPENDOUS "SMOKE" RINGS

Objective: To produce amazing "smoke" rings using dry ice.

Materials:
- Dry Ice
- Insulated gloves
- 20 oz plastic soft drink bottle

Safety Precautions: Use dry ice only with adult supervision. Never touch dry ice with your bare skin – it may cause frostbite! Use dry ice only outdoors or in a well-ventilated room to prevent buildup of carbon dioxide gas. Do not inhale vapors – inhalation of vapors may cause suffocation, since carbon dioxide displaces oxygen.

Procedure:
1. Fill a plastic soft drink bottle about halfway with warm water and add a chunk of dry ice. Under no circumstances should the cap be replaced.
2. Holding the bottle at a slight angle, give it a good squeeze. Beautiful "smoke" rings will be produced!

Explanation: The rings produced are not really smoke, but rather tiny droplets of liquid water or fog. A better name for what is produced would be fog rings. They will always be round, because like a bubble, the rings represent a position of minimum energy. In other words, it takes the least amount of energy for the rings to form in this fashion. When the fog is forced from the bottle, it expands due to the reduced pressure of the air outside the bottle, leaving a hollow area in the center and producing a beautiful ring.

Imagine a container where the opening through which the "smoke" travels is a shape other than circular. Suppose it was a triangular or square opening. Would the rings produced be of this shape, or would they still be round?

Experiment # 13:
A CASCADING WATER FOUNTAIN

Objective: To create a cascading water fountain using dry ice.

Materials:

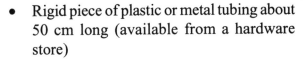

- Dry Ice
- Insulated gloves
- 20 oz plastic soda bottle with cap
- Electric drill
- Rigid piece of plastic or metal tubing about 50 cm long (available from a hardware store)

Safety Precautions: Use dry ice only with adult supervision. Never touch dry ice with your bare skin – it may cause frostbite! Use dry ice only outdoors or in a well-ventilated room to prevent buildup of carbon dioxide gas. Do not inhale vapors – inhalation of vapors may cause suffocation, since carbon dioxide displaces oxygen.

Procedure:
1. Drill a hole in the top of the bottle cap so

that the piece of tubing will fit snugly.

2. Extend the tubing down into the empty bottle until it is nearly touching the bottom.

3. Fill the bottle about halfway with water, add a piece of dry ice, and then screw on the cap with the tubing through it. You will immediately witness a cascading fountain of water flowing out of the top of the tubing until the bottle is nearly empty.

Explanation: As the dry ice sublimes due to being placed in the water, the space above the water fills with carbon dioxide gas. Therefore the pressure on top of the water increases. This increasing pressure will force the water up and out of the tubing until nearly all of the water has been emptied from the bottle. Anytime pressure is applied to the surface of a liquid, that pressure is transmitted equally to all points within the liquid. This principle enables drinking straws and barometers to function, with atmospheric pressure pushing down on the surface of the liquid. With the fountain that you built, the pressure that builds up due to the sublimating dry ice is much greater than atmospheric pressure.

Experiment # 14:
THE EXPANDING BAG

Objective: To discover how much volume a piece of dry ice will occupy as it sublimates.

Materials:

- Dry Ice
- Insulated gloves
- Gallon size freezer bag
- Latex rubber glove
- Large balloon

Safety Precautions: The bag, balloon, or glove may burst open if too large of a piece of dry ice is used – use a piece no larger than a marble. Place the bag, balloon, or glove at least 3 meters away after adding the dry ice. Wear safety goggles. Use dry ice only with adult supervision. Never touch dry ice with your bare skin – it may cause frostbite! Use dry ice only outdoors or in a well-ventilated room to prevent buildup of carbon dioxide gas. Do not inhale vapors – inhalation of vapors may cause suffocation, since carbon dioxide displaces oxygen.

Procedure:

1. Place a piece of dry ice no larger than a marble in a gallon size freezer bag.

2. Seal the bag and then place the bag about 3 meters away. You may also do the same thing with a latex rubber glove or a large balloon. Simply add a marble-size piece of dry ice, tie it off, and then place a safe distance away as you watch it expand.
3. Once all off the dry ice has sublimed, it is safe to observe the CO_2 filled bag up close.

Explanation: As the dry ice sublimates, it will cause the bag to expand, until the dry ice is completely gone and you are left with a bag filled with CO_2.

If you have taken high school chemistry, you know that 1 mole of any gas occupies a volume of 22.4 liters at STP (standard temperature and pressure: 1 atm at 0°C). How much dry ice would you need to use in order to have 22.4 L of CO_2 gas? (Since 1 mole of dry ice has a mass of 44 grams, then 44 g of dry ice would sublimate to form 22.4 L of CO_2 gas at STP.)

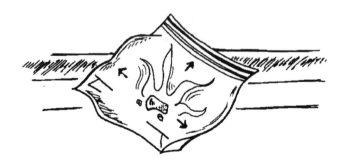

Experiment # 15:

ILLUMINATING LASER BEAMS

Objective: To observe laser beams using the fog produced from dry ice.

Materials:
- Dry Ice
- Insulated gloves
- Large bowl or basin
- Laser

Safety Precautions: *Never look directly at a laser or point it at another person's eyes. Permanent eye damage may result.* Use dry ice only with adult supervision. Never touch dry ice with your bare skin – it may cause frostbite! Use dry ice only outdoors or in a well-ventilated room to prevent buildup of carbon dioxide gas. Do not inhale vapors – inhalation of vapors may cause suffocation, since carbon dioxide displaces oxygen.

Procedure:
1. This experiment is best performed at night so that you can better view the laser beams. Place some warm water from the tap into

a large bowl and add some chunks of dry ice. You will immediately see a copious amount of fog produced.

2. Turn out the lights and shine your laser through the fog. The entire laser beam will be clearly visible!

Explanation: It is common in the movies to see scenes in which characters illuminate a laser beam with an aerosol spray or some type of dust. The same effect is occurring with the fog from the dry ice. The laser beam is bouncing off each particle of water, making the beam visible. You can also say that the laser beam is being scattered by the particles of water in the fog. This scattering is known as the Tyndall Effect, and can also be observed when a laser is projected through any colloid. A colloid is a suspension of one type of particle in another. Fog, clouds, and milk are common examples of colloids. They generally have a cloudy appearance, as opposed to a solution, which is always transparent. Colloids tend to be cloudy because the particles are much larger than those in a solution. It is these relatively large particles that scatter light and make laser beams visible.

Experiment # 16:
FORMING CARBONATED WATER

Objective: To form carbonated water and to record its pH.

Materials:

- Dry Ice
- Insulated gloves
- Clean plastic cup or glass
- pH paper (available from a hobby store or your local science teacher)

Safety Precautions: Use dry ice only with adult supervision. Never touch dry ice with your bare skin – it may cause frostbite! Use dry ice only outdoors or in a well-ventilated room to prevent buildup of carbon dioxide gas. Do not inhale vapors – inhalation of vapors may cause suffocation, since carbon dioxide displaces oxygen.

Procedure:

1. Fill a clean cup or glass with water and record its pH with a piece of pH paper. Do this by pouring a small amount of water into another container and then dipping the pH paper into it. Do not dip the pH paper

directly into the cup of water, since you will drink it later.

2. Now add a piece of dry ice to the water. When it has completely sublimated, take a drink. How does it taste? Is the water colder? Wait until the dry ice has completely sublimated before drinking, in order to avoid having a piece of dry ice touch your lips or tongue.

3. After you have tasted it, test its pH. What has happened to the pH?

Explanation: As you may recall from experiment 9, when CO_2 is added to water, carbonic acid is formed. This is also known as carbonated water. Although most acids taste sour, carbonated water tends to taste bitter, at least to some people. You should also notice a definite drop in pH, to around 5 or 6.

Another use of dry ice is to re-carbonate soda that has gone flat. The next time you find some left over soda in the refrigerator, simply pour it in a glass and add a piece of dry ice. When the dry ice has disappeared, drink up! You can also try carbonating orange juice or other beverages using dry ice.

Experiment # 17:
THE LEAKY FAUCET

Objective: To demonstrate that bubbles filled with CO_2 are denser than air.

Materials:

- Dry Ice
- Insulated gloves
- Eight foot length of 3/4 inch PVC pipe
- Two 90° 3/4 inch PVC elbow connectors
- Hack saw
- Tornado tube (available from a toy or hobby shop)
- Duct tape
- 2-Liter bottle
- Hot water
- Bubble solution (either buy commercially or squirt some dishwashing liquid in water)

Safety Precautions: Use dry ice only with adult supervision. Never touch dry ice with your bare skin – it may cause frostbite! Use dry ice only outdoors or in a well-ventilated room to prevent buildup of carbon dioxide gas. Do not inhale vapors – inhalation of vapors may cause suffocation, since carbon dioxide displaces oxygen.

Procedure:

1. Using a hack saw, cut the PVC pipe into three sections of the following lengths: 6 feet, 15 inches, and 4 inches.

2. Connect the 6-foot section with the 15-inch section using an elbow. Then connect the other elbow to the other end of the 15-inch section.

3. Connect the 4-inch section to this elbow so that it is pointing down. (See illustration on page 56.)

4. To the other end of the 6-foot section, securely attach a tornado tube using duct tape.

5. Pour about 200 mL of very hot water into the bottle, add several pieces of dry ice, and then quickly screw the tornado tube into the 2-Liter bottle. It helps to have two people to do this experiment – one to hold the PVC pipe and the other to hold the bottle. You should now see a steady stream of fog pouring downward from the small piece of tubing.

6. Quickly place the container of bubble solution over the end of the small piece of PVC pipe. As you remove the container, there should be a bubble film extending over the tubing. As the CO_2 pours out of the tube, it will form a bubble, which will be followed by others in quick succession, all rapidly falling to the ground! Try to

catch a bubble in your hand. See if you can get a bubble to bounce off the tabletop.

Explanation: This experiment is fascinating to watch. It is awe-inspiring to watch the bubbles so quickly form, fall, and then burst with a sudden release of fog. This experiment demonstrates many important principles. It first of all shows clearly just what a bubble is: a very thin spherical membrane of soap that is filled with a gas. Bubbles will always assume a spherical shape, since this is the position of greatest stability.

This experiment also demonstrates that CO_2 gas is denser than air. A denser gas will always sink in a less dense gas, because the force of gravity acting downward on the denser gas is greater than the buoyant force of the lighter gas pushing upward. Therefore, the CO_2 filled bubbles fall quickly to the ground.

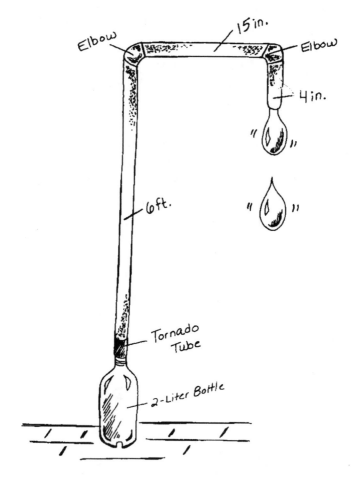

Elbow

15 in.

Elbow

4 in.

" ("O") "

6 ft.

" ("O") "

Tornado Tube

2-Liter Bottle

(diagram of leaky faucet apparatus)

Experiment # 18:
DRY ICE CRYSTAL BALL

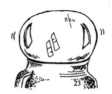

Objective: To use dry ice to make a huge bubble resembling a crystal ball.

Materials:

- Dry Ice
- Insulated gloves
- One gallon aquarium, bucket, or other container of similar dimensions
- Soap solution (use a commercial bubble solution or squirt some dishwashing detergent into water)
- A cotton rag that is longer than the diameter of the container

Safety Precautions: Use dry ice only with adult supervision. Never touch dry ice with your bare skin – it may cause frostbite! Use dry ice only outdoors or in a well-ventilated room to prevent buildup of carbon dioxide gas. Do not inhale vapors – inhalation of vapors may cause suffocation, since carbon dioxide displaces oxygen.

Procedure:

1. Fill the container about half full with water. Add several large pieces of dry ice.
2. Dip the rag in the bubble solution, allow any excess solution to drip off, and then roll the rag up loosely.
3. Pull the soapy rag over the top of the container until it forms a thin soap film over the entire surface. As the dry ice continues to sublimate and release gas, the bubble will grow in size until it becomes huge – resembling a crystal ball!
4. Try using containers of different shapes. What shape do you think the resulting bubble will be?

Explanation: The technique will require some practice. If too much dry ice is added or the water is too warm, vapor will be produced too quickly, popping the bubble film before it has a chance to expand. Also, if soap is accidentally dripped into the large container, soap suds will form, which will interfere with the formation of the "crystal ball."

This experiment demonstrates how bubbles are formed, and their extraordinary capacity to assume very large sizes if the conditions are right. Experiment with larger containers to see how big of a bubble you can produce using this method.

Experiment # 19:
HOMEMADE ROOT BEER

Objective: To make delicious, refreshing root beer using dry ice.

Materials:
- Dry Ice
- Insulated gloves
- Sugar
- Root beer concentrate (available from some grocery stores)
- Cup
- Plastic coffee stirrer
- Eyedropper

Safety Precautions: Do not drink the root beer until all of the dry ice has sublimated. Use dry ice only with adult supervision. Never touch dry ice with your bare skin -- it may cause frostbite! Use dry ice only outdoors or in a well-ventilated room to prevent buildup of carbon dioxide gas. Do not inhale vapors – inhalation of vapors may cause suffocation, since carbon dioxide displaces oxygen.

Procedure:
1. In a plastic cup, place 17 drops of root beer

concentrate and 21 grams of sugar (about 4 level teaspoonfuls).

2. Add about 240 mL (8 oz) of water to the cup and stir until most of the sugar and root beer concentrate have dissolved.

3. Now add a chunk of dry ice. Do not drink the root beer until the dry ice has completely sublimed. When it has, enjoy a cold refreshing glass of homemade root beer!

Explanation: The dry ice serves to carbonate the root beer by adding carbon dioxide. This makes the root beer slightly acidic, and also serves to give it a "fizz." The instructions on the container of root beer concentrate will most likely call for the use of yeast to produce carbon dioxide. But dry ice works just as well!

Carbonated drinks are made by adding carbon dioxide gas under high pressure at the bottling plant. It is the addition of CO_2 that gives soft drinks their fizz. Another name for carbonic acid is carbonated water, which is often the first ingredient listed on the label of a carbonated beverage.

Experiment # 20:
A MINIATURE TORNADO

Objective: To create a mini-tornado using dry ice.

Materials:

- Dry Ice
- Insulated gloves
- Box fan
- Vacuum cleaner

Safety Precautions: Use dry ice only with adult supervision. Never touch dry ice with your bare skin – it may cause frostbite! Use dry ice only outdoors or in a well-ventilated room to prevent buildup of carbon dioxide gas. Do not inhale vapors – inhalation of vapors may cause suffocation, since carbon dioxide displaces oxygen.

Procedure:

1. Place a block of dry ice on the floor. Place a box fan about 6 meters away so that it blows directly across the block of dry ice.
2. Turn the vacuum cleaner on, place the hose a few centimeters above the block of dry ice, and then gradually move the hose

upward until it is about 15 cm above the surface. You will see tiny tornadoes lift off from the surface of the dry ice and disappear within the vacuum cleaner hose. Some of these may only last for a few seconds, but the formation of a vortex can be easily observed with a little patience.

Explanation: Although the exact mechanism by which tornadoes form is still not completely understood, there are several conditions which must be met in order for a tornado to occur. Tornadoes are always accompanied by a front, which involves the movement of air in a horizontal direction. This is simulated by the fan.

If a cold front collides with a warm front, the cold air will push the warm air upward. This creates an updraft. The updraft in our experiment is created by the vacuum cleaner. The rate of sublimation of dry ice is greatly increased when air pressure above it is reduced by the vacuum cleaner, enhancing the visibility of the vortex. The fog produced by the sublimating dry ice is due to the rapid cooling of the air around the dry ice, resulting in water vapor from the air condensing, forming tiny water droplets. Tornadoes usually spin counterclockwise in the northern hemisphere and clockwise in the southern hemisphere. In which direction did your vortex spin?

Experiment # 21:
WILL DRY ICE KEEP YOUR DRINK COLD?

Objective: To discover whether dry ice is more effective than ordinary ice at cooling a liquid.

Materials:

- Dry Ice
- Insulated gloves
- Two thermometers
- Two Styrofoam cups
- Ice cube
- Sensitive balance

Safety Precautions: Use dry ice only with adult supervision. Never touch dry ice with your bare skin – it may cause frostbite! Use dry ice only outdoors or in a well-ventilated room to prevent buildup of carbon dioxide gas. Do not inhale vapors – inhalation of vapors may cause suffocation, since carbon dioxide displaces oxygen.

Procedure:

1. Fill two Styrofoam cups with equal amounts of hot water from the tap. Place a thermometer in each.
2. Add a regular ice cube to one cup and a

piece of dry ice of the same mass to the other cup. Using a pencil, keep the regular ice cube submerged, since the piece of dry ice will sink to the bottom of the cup.

3. As soon as the ice cube melts, record the final temperature of the water.

4. As soon as the piece of dry ice has completely sublimated, record the final temperature of the water. How does the temperature in the two cups compare?

Explanation: Anytime ice melts – or sublimates – energy is taken in from the surroundings. That is why adding ice to your drink makes it cold – the melting of ice requires energy, and the transfer of energy from your drink to the ice cube lowers the temperature of the drink. Dry ice does the same thing. In order to sublimate, energy must be absorbed. The heat required to melt ordinary ice is known as the heat of fusion. It takes about 334 Joules (J) of energy to melt a gram of ice. (There are 4.18 Joules in 1 calorie.) The heat required to cause the sublimation of dry ice is known as the heat of sublimation. It takes about 573 J of energy to sublimate 1 gram of dry ice. The large discrepancy accounts for dry ice's greater effectiveness – relative to normal ice – in cooling a drink.

Experiment # 22:
DO OIL AND DRY ICE MIX?

Objective: To discover what happens when dry ice is added to vegetable oil.

Materials:

- Dry Ice
- Insulated gloves
- Transparent plastic cup
- Vegetable oil
- Corn syrup

Safety Precautions: Use dry ice only with adult supervision. Never touch dry ice with your bare skin – it may cause frostbite! Use dry ice only outdoors or in a well-ventilated room to prevent buildup of carbon dioxide gas. Do not inhale vapors – inhalation of vapors may cause suffocation, since carbon dioxide displaces oxygen.

Procedure:
1. Pour some vegetable oil into a cup. Add a piece of dry ice. Make sure you have enough oil so that the piece of dry ice is completely submerged. Observe what happens.

2. Now add some water to the cup. The water will immediately sink to the bottom of the cup. You will notice the oil filling with beautiful bubbles.
3. Now add some corn syrup. What happens to it? Does the dry ice sink or float on this layer?

Explanation: When the dry ice is added to the oil, sublimation occurs as evidenced by the bubbles. However, very little fog is produced. When water is added, it immediately sinks because it is denser than the oil. The oil then becomes filled with bubbles. These bubbles are composed of tiny droplets of water that have been pulled up by the sublimating dry ice. Since water and oil do not mix, these bubbles are very noticeable. You will also notice the formation of a cloud above the cup after the water was added. This cloud was barely visible when the dry ice was added to just the oil. This proves that the cloud produced when dry ice is added to water is due to tiny droplets of water that are pulled out by the rapidly escaping carbon dioxide. Tiny water droplets also make up the clouds and fog that are produced naturally.

Experiment # 23:
A RUBBER BAND SNAKE

Objective: To discover the effects of low temperature on a rubber band.

Materials:
- Dry Ice
- Insulated gloves
- Thick rubber band
- Hammer

Safety Precautions: Use dry ice only with adult supervision. Never touch dry ice with your bare skin – it may cause frostbite! Use dry ice only outdoors or in a well-ventilated room to prevent buildup of carbon dioxide gas. Do not inhale vapors – inhalation of vapors may cause suffocation, since carbon dioxide displaces oxygen.

Procedure:
1. Wearing insulated gloves, tightly wrap a thick rubber band several times around a small block of dry ice. The rubber band must be very tightly bound around the piece of dry ice.
2. After about 15 minutes, break the chunk

of ice with a hammer, until the rubber band is completely free of the ice. The rubber band will maintain its same shape, even though it is no longer in contact with the dry ice. After a few seconds, the rubber band will begin to unravel, resembling the uncoiling of a snake.

Explanation: As the rubber band becomes cold, its molecules slow down. This makes the rubber very brittle, causing it to maintain the shape of the block of dry ice even when the dry ice is removed. As the rubber band warms, its molecules speed up again, causing the rubber band to become flexible and to unravel.

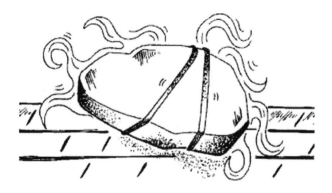

Experiment # 24:
FREEZING FLOWER PETALS

Objective: To demonstrate the effects of very low temperatures on a flower.

Materials:

- Dry Ice
- Insulated gloves
- Acetone (available from the hardware store)
- Metal bowl
- Fresh flowers

Safety Precautions: Acetone is flammable – keep away from open flames. Do not inhale acetone vapors, as they are harmful to your health. Do not allow acetone to come into contact with your skin. Use dry ice only with adult supervision. Never touch dry ice with your bare skin – it may cause frostbite! Use dry ice only outdoors or in a well-ventilated room to prevent buildup of carbon dioxide gas. Do not inhale vapors – inhalation of vapors may cause suffocation, since carbon dioxide displaces oxygen.

Procedure:

1. Pour about 500 mL of acetone into a metal bowl. To this add several large chunks of dry ice. At first the acetone will bubble vigorously, but then will settle down and become fairly calm.
2. After a few minutes, submerge some flowers into the solution. Leave them in for several minutes.
3. When you remove them, smash them on the tabletop. They will have become very brittle and will shatter like glass.

Explanation: Acetone has a very low freezing point. The dry ice is not cold enough to cause it to freeze. But the addition of dry ice will still lower its temperature dramatically. This extremely low temperature will cause the flower petals to become very brittle, enabling them to be shattered quite easily.

Experiment # 25:
MICROWAVES AND DRY ICE

Objective: To discover the effect of microwaves on a piece of dry ice.

Materials:

- Dry Ice
- Insulated gloves
- Microwaveable plates
- Microwaveable cups
- Ice cube

Safety Precautions: Use dry ice only with adult supervision. Never touch dry ice with your bare skin – it may cause frostbite! Use dry ice only outdoors or in a well-ventilated room to prevent buildup of carbon dioxide gas. Do not inhale vapors – inhalation of vapors may cause suffocation, since carbon dioxide displaces oxygen.

Procedure:

1. Put an ice cube on a plate and place the plate in the microwave oven. Next to this, place a beaker or cup of water. (The beaker of water will serve to prevent damage to your oven by absorbing stray microwaves.)

2. Turn on the microwave for 1 minute. What happens to the ice?
3. Repeat this same experiment with dry ice. What happens to the dry ice?

Explanation: Microwaves interact with different substances in different ways. Some substances, such as metals, reflect microwaves, causing sparks. Other substances, such as glass, allow microwaves to pass through without themselves being warmed. Still other substances, most notably water, absorb microwaves. This absorption of energy by water molecules makes them move back and forth very rapidly, producing molecular friction, which generates heat.

In order to heat food in the microwave oven, the food must contain water or it will not get warm. Even though regular ice does not very efficiently absorb microwave radiation, a fine layer of liquid water on its surface absorbs the microwave energy very well. As this layer of water becomes heated, its heat is transferred to the ice beneath it, causing it to melt.

Dry ice does not absorb microwaves. Therefore, placing a chunk of dry ice in the microwave oven will have little effect on its rate of sublimation. When you remove the dry ice from the oven, it will be roughly the same size as when you inserted it.

Experiment # 26:
CAN DRY ICE FREEZE WATER?

Objective: To discover whether or not dry ice is capable of freezing water.

Materials:

- Dry Ice
- Insulated gloves
- Disposable plastic cup

Safety Precautions: Use dry ice only with adult supervision. Never touch dry ice with your bare skin – it may cause frostbite! Use dry ice only outdoors or in a well-ventilated room to prevent buildup of carbon dioxide gas. Do not inhale vapors – inhalation of vapors may cause suffocation, since carbon dioxide displaces oxygen.

Procedure:

1. Place a large chunk of dry ice in a plastic cup.
2. Add water to the cup and also pour some water on the tabletop under the cup. You should have approximately a 2:1 ratio by volume of dry ice to water.
3. Observe for 10 – 15 minutes. The water

will freeze solid, and the cup will freeze to the tabletop. You will be able to hear a hissing sound as the carbon dioxide gas escapes from within the ice.

Explanation: Since the dry ice is much colder than water, energy will be transferred from the water to the dry ice. Eventually, the water will lose so much energy that it will freeze. You will then have a layer of normal ice surrounding the dry ice. Remember that water freezes at 0°C, but dry ice "freezes" at -78.5°C. The dry ice is still sublimating, however, so you can hear a loud hissing sound as the carbon dioxide gas creates holes and fissures in the ice from which to escape.

You can also fill a plastic soda bottle about halfway with water and submerge it in a cooler filled with dry ice. (Do not place dry ice directly in the bottle!) How long does it take for the water to freeze solid?

Experiment # 27:
MAKING A "SUPER SOAKER"

Objective: To construct a very powerful "squirt gun" using dry ice.

Materials:
- Dry Ice
- Insulated gloves
- Electric drill
- 2-Liter bottle

Safety Precautions: Use dry ice only with adult supervision. Never touch dry ice with your bare skin – it may cause frostbite! Use dry ice only outdoors or in a well-ventilated room to prevent buildup of carbon dioxide gas. Do not inhale vapors – inhalation of vapors may cause suffocation, since carbon dioxide displaces oxygen.

Procedure:
1. Using an electric drill, carefully drill a hole in the top of a 2-Liter bottle cap. The size is not crucial, but it should be at least 3 mm in diameter.
2. Fill the 2-Liter bottle nearly full with water, add a chunk of dry ice, and screw on the

cap with the hole.

3. Turn the bottle horizontally and witness the powerful flow of water from the hole. As the water level drops, you will need to tilt the bottle in such a way that water is in contact with the cap. If held upside down, the water will be forced out of the hole very rapidly. This experiment is best done outdoors, since it will make quite a mess!

Explanation: As the dry ice sublimates, it releases carbon dioxide gas. This gas exerts pressure on the surface of the water, forcing water out of the hole. Super soaker squirt guns operate in a similar fashion, using compressed air to put pressure on the water.

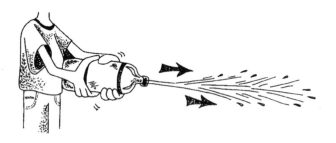

Experiment # 28:
A SODA FOUNTAIN

Objective: To make a tremendous soda fountain using dry ice.

Materials:

- Dry Ice
- Insulated gloves
- 2-Liter bottle of soda

Safety Precautions: Use dry ice only with adult supervision. Never touch dry ice with your bare skin – it may cause frostbite! Use dry ice only outdoors or in a well-ventilated room to prevent buildup of carbon dioxide gas. Do not inhale vapors – inhalation of vapors may cause suffocation, since carbon dioxide displaces oxygen.

Procedure:

1. Open a new 2-Liter bottle of soda (diet root beer works especially well) that is at room temperature.
2. Drop in a piece of dry ice.
3. Stand back! You will witness a tremendous fountain of soda shoot up into the air and then quickly come cascading back down. (This experiment is best done

outdoors or in the kitchen sink since it will involve the overflow of a substantial amount of soda.)

Explanation: When the dry ice is dropped into the warm soda, it begins to immediately sublimate very rapidly. This rapid sublimation releases carbon dioxide gas. This carbon dioxide gas produces many new sites for molecules of carbon dioxide gas that are already in the soda to adhere to. When enough molecules congregate in one place so as to be visible, bubbles form. These bubbles quickly rise to the surface of the bottle, bringing with them a tremendous amount of soda.

When the cap is removed from the 2-Liter bottle of soda, the sudden pressure drop causes many carbon dioxide molecules to come out of solution. Bubbles form when carbon dioxide molecules that have come out of solution clump together in a large enough quantity to form a visible entity. However, only a limited number of bubbles can form if the carbon dioxide molecules have nothing to adhere to. Adding anything to soda will cause more bubbles to form. The next time you add an ice cube to a glass of soda, note the increase in fizzing. Adding salt to soda will cause a great deal of fizzing as well, since the salt particles create many nucleation sites that enable bubbles to form. A nucleation site provides a place for bubbles of carbon dioxide gas to adhere.

For further verification of this phenomenon, pour two glasses of freshly poured soda. Add dry ice to one and let the other serve as a control. When the dry ice has completely sublimated, take a sip of each. You might expect the glass of soda with the dry ice added to have the most fizz. But is this the case? If not, can you explain why?

Experiment # 29:
CUTTING A BLOCK OF DRY ICE IN HALF

Objective: To discover whether a piece of dry ice can be sliced in half by applying pressure.

Materials:
- Dry Ice
- Insulated gloves
- Clipboard with metal clip

Safety Precautions: Use dry ice only with adult supervision. Never touch dry ice with your bare skin – it may cause frostbite! Use dry ice only outdoors or in a well-ventilated room to prevent buildup of carbon dioxide gas. Do not inhale vapors – inhalation of vapors may cause suffocation, since carbon dioxide displaces oxygen.

Procedure:
Obtain a piece of dry ice that will fit under the metal clip of a clipboard. Allow the clip to rest on top of the piece of dry ice. In several minutes, the clip will have completely passed through the chunk of dry ice, cutting it in half!

Explanation: Although it may seem that pressure is primarily responsible for the effect you have just observed, this is not the case. To test this idea, try applying pressure on a piece of dry ice with the edge of a plastic credit card. It will be much more difficult to slice the piece of dry ice in half than with a piece of metal, even if the same amount of pressure is applied to each. Why? The answer lies in how well each substance can conduct heat.

Metals are excellent conductors of heat, whereas plastics are not. As a result, a piece of metal at room temperature will very readily transfer its energy as heat to the piece of dry ice, causing the dry ice in contact with the metal to sublimate very rapidly. As a result, the piece of dry ice is cut in half. Plastics, on the other hand, are good insulators and poor conductors. They tend to hold in their energy, transferring it very slowly to their surroundings. Think about what utensil you use when stirring a pan of boiling water. You will probably use plastic or wood, since it will not heat up as quickly as will a metal utensil.

During this experiment, you will also notice a layer of frost forming on the metal clip of the clipboard. This demonstrates that a tremendous amount of heat has been transferred from the metal to the dry ice, causing a large drop in the temperature of the metal. This causes water vapor to condense from the air and deposit into frost on the metal clip.

Experiment # 30:
HOW DENSE IS DRY ICE?

Objective: To discover the density of dry ice.

Materials:

- Dry Ice
- Insulated gloves
- Digital balance
- Graduated cylinder or measuring cup
- Plastic cup

Safety Precautions: Use dry ice only with adult supervision. Never touch dry ice with your bare skin – it may cause frostbite! Use dry ice only outdoors or in a well-ventilated room to prevent buildup of carbon dioxide gas. Do not inhale vapors – inhalation of vapors may cause suffocation, since carbon dioxide displaces oxygen.

Procedure:

1. To determine the density of a piece of dry ice, you must measure its mass and its volume. You will need to work fast, since the dry ice sublimates rapidly. Determine its mass by placing the piece of dry ice on

a sensitive balance.
2. Determine its volume by water displacement. Fill a plastic cup to the brim with water and then place this cup in a shallow pie pan. Place the piece of dry ice in the cup. Some water will overflow in the pan.
3. Pour the water that overflowed into a graduated cylinder or measuring cup to determine its volume.

Explanation: Density is a comparison of the mass of a substance to its volume. It is normally measured in grams per milliliter (g/mL). If two objects have the same volume, yet different masses, the substance with the greater mass will have the greater density. Lead and gold, for example, are very dense, whereas air and helium are much less dense. The formula for density is mass divided by volume ($D = M/V$).

If you take the mass of your sample of dry ice in grams and divide it by its volume in mL, you will have its density. You no doubt have noticed that dry ice sinks in water. The density of water is 1 g/mL. Is your calculated density of dry ice greater or less than this? The accepted density of dry ice is 1.5 g/mL. How close were you to this value?

Experiment # 31:
THE WHISTLING TEAKETTLE

Objective: To observe the sound made when a gas travels through a small hole.

Materials:

- Dry Ice
- Insulated gloves
- Teakettle

Safety Precautions: Use dry ice only with adult supervision. Never touch dry ice with your bare skin – it may cause frostbite! Use dry ice only outdoors or in a well-ventilated room to prevent buildup of carbon dioxide gas. Do not inhale vapors – inhalation of vapors may cause suffocation, since carbon dioxide displaces oxygen.

Procedure:

1. Fill a teakettle about halfway with warm water.
2. Add several chunks of dry ice.
3. After a short time, note the whistling of the teakettle.

Explanation: The whistling of a teakettle generally signals the boiling of water as steam is expelled from the small hole in the spout. But no boiling occurs in this experiment. As dry ice is added to water, it sublimates, forming CO_2 gas. The gas being expelled from the hole in the spout creates the familiar whistling sound. However, the water is not boiling but is very cold!

Experiment # 32:
MAKING A COMET

Objective: To construct a replica of a comet using dry ice.

Materials:
- Dry Ice
- Insulated gloves
- Sand
- Ammonia
- Corn syrup
- Bucket
- Large wooden spoon or paint stirrer
- Large plastic garbage bag
- Measuring cup

Safety Precautions: Ammonia is very poisonous – do not inhale vapors. Use dry ice only with adult supervision. Never touch dry ice with your bare skin – it may cause frostbite! Use dry ice only outdoors or in a well-ventilated room to prevent buildup of carbon dioxide gas. Do not inhale vapors – inhalation of vapors may cause suffocation, since carbon dioxide displaces oxygen.

Procedure:
1. In a bucket, place 2 cups of dry ice that

have been crushed up into small pieces with a hammer.

2. Add 2 cups of water, 50 mL of sand, 10 mL of ammonia, and 10 mL of corn syrup. Mix thoroughly.

3. When thoroughly mixed and somewhat slushy, pour onto a trash bag that has been flattened out. Wearing your gloves, mold the contents into a ball, being sure the plastic stays between your gloves and the mixture. The contents will freeze into a ball very quickly, and will remain intact. You have formed an instant comet, with gas jets spewing out in various places.

Explanation: Comets are celestial bodies that orbit the sun. They are essentially a "dirty snowball," consisting of dust and ice, roughly similar in composition to the comet you constructed (except for the corn syrup, which has the primary purpose of holding the ingredients together). The tail of a comet becomes more visible as it approaches the sun, due to the heat increasing the rate of sublimation of the ice that makes up the comet. The expelling gas jets in your comet represent the tail.

The head of a comet can be as large as the planet Jupiter, but usually they are only a few cubic kilometers in volume. The tail, however, can be from 50 million to 80 million kilometers long.

Experiment # 33:
FREEZING OBJECTS WITH DRY ICE

Objective: To observe the effect of extreme cold on different substances.

Materials:

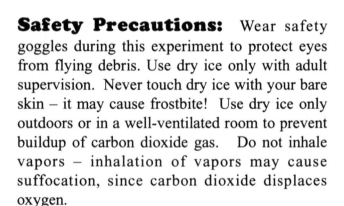

- Dry Ice
- Insulated gloves
- Apple, banana, and other food items
- Tennis ball
- Racquet ball

Safety Precautions: Wear safety goggles during this experiment to protect eyes from flying debris. Use dry ice only with adult supervision. Never touch dry ice with your bare skin – it may cause frostbite! Use dry ice only outdoors or in a well-ventilated room to prevent buildup of carbon dioxide gas. Do not inhale vapors – inhalation of vapors may cause suffocation, since carbon dioxide displaces oxygen.

Procedure:

1. This experiment works best if you can obtain dry ice in pellet form. If not, break

into pieces with a hammer. Submerge an apple in a cooler of dry ice and leave it undisturbed for about 30 minutes.

2. Wearing gloves, remove the apple and drop it on a hard floor, or hit it with a hammer. What happens to it?

3. Repeat with hot dogs, bananas, or other food items. Try the same procedure with a tennis ball or a racquetball. Always wear safety goggles to protect your eyes. What effect does cold have on these objects?

Explanation: The -78.5°C temperature produced by the dry ice has an extreme effect on many substances. It can severely damage living tissue – causing frostbite. It can also make ordinary items like apples and balls so brittle that they shatter like glass. One reason a substance like an apple will become brittle is that all of the water contained within it has turned to ice. You know very well that an icicle will shatter if dropped on a hard floor. As for substances that do not contain water, such as a racquetball, the brittleness is due to the fact that molecules tend to slow down when they are cooled. As these molecules slow down, the bonds between them become considerably weaker, causing substances to lose much of their elasticity and become brittle.

Experiment # 34:
MAKING A MINIATURE SUBMARINE

Objective: To make a miniature submarine which will ascend of its own accord.

Materials:

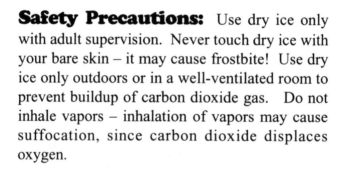

- Dry Ice
- Insulated gloves
- Film canister
- Electric drill
- Tall graduated cylinder or 2-Liter bottle

Safety Precautions: Use dry ice only with adult supervision. Never touch dry ice with your bare skin – it may cause frostbite! Use dry ice only outdoors or in a well-ventilated room to prevent buildup of carbon dioxide gas. Do not inhale vapors – inhalation of vapors may cause suffocation, since carbon dioxide displaces oxygen.

Procedure:

1. Using an electric drill, drill a small hole no more than 4 mm in diameter in the lid of the film canister.
2. Fill a large graduated cylinder nearly to the top with water. If you do not have a

cylinder, cut off the top from a 2-Liter bottle so that the canister may fit inside.

3. Now add some water to the canister and drop in a chunk of dry ice. Replace the lid and drop the canister lid side down into the cylinder of water. The canister should drop straight to the bottom at this point. If it does not, then add more water or more dry ice until it does. You will immediately notice bubbles rising from the hole in the canister.

4. After a short period of time, the canister will rise back up to the surface. Will the submarine work using only dry ice and no water? What if the hole is facing upward instead of downward? Try these variations.

Explanation: The canister initially sinks because when filled with water and dry ice it has a density greater than that of the water. As the dry ice sublimates, carbon dioxide gas is formed. This gas forces the water out of the canister. In addition, sublimation shrinks the size of the dry ice. As a result of these two factors, the density of the mini-submarine eventually becomes less than that of the surrounding water, and it rises to the top, being buoyed up by the water. Real submarines operate under the same principle. To submerge, they take on water in their ballast tanks, which makes them denser than water. To ascend, they release water, making them less dense.

Experiment # 35:
THE OOZING CAN OF SODA

Objective: To observe the effects of extreme cold on a can of soda.

Materials:

- Dry Ice
- Insulated gloves
- Can of soda

Safety Precautions: Use dry ice only with adult supervision. Never touch dry ice with your bare skin – it may cause frostbite! Use dry ice only outdoors or in a well-ventilated room to prevent buildup of carbon dioxide gas. Do not inhale vapors – inhalation of vapors may cause suffocation, since carbon dioxide displaces oxygen.

Procedure:

1. Place a can of soda in a cooler of dry ice so that it is completely submerged. Dry ice in pellet form works best. If not available, break up the dry ice using a hammer.
2. Check on the can of soda every 5 minutes.

It is imperative that it does not freeze solid, or else it will expand and burst, making a big mess. Your goal is for the contents of the can to freeze only partially. This will make the can very firm and slightly extended, with no sound heard when shaken. At this point, remove the can from the dry ice and place it in the kitchen sink or outdoors.

3. Now open the can. You will see a thick, frothy foam spew out until the can is nearly empty. If nothing happens when the can is opened, it was probably left in the dry ice for too long.

Explanation: You may have already noticed this phenomenon if you have ever tried to cool a can of soda quickly by placing it in the freezer. If you leave it in too long, an incredible outpouring of soda occurs upon opening, causing you to lose the majority of the contents. As liquids get cooler, more gas can be dissolved in them. However, as liquids freeze into solids, any dissolved gases are forced out, since gases are not very soluble in solids. Therefore, as the soda begins to freeze, the dissolved carbon dioxide (which provides the fizz in soda) is forced out.

Obviously, a can of soda will not freeze all at once. Therefore there is a very high concentration of carbon dioxide gas in the thick, viscous liquid that has not yet frozen. That explains why for this experiment it is important that the contents be only partially frozen. That way there is a very large concentration of CO_2 in the liquid. When the can of soda is opened, the CO_2 gas is now under reduced pressure, so it begins to expand considerably, bringing with it a great deal of the sticky, frothy, viscous liquid.

Experiment # 36:

A DRY ICE POWERED BOAT

Objective: To make a boat that is propelled by dry ice.

Materials:
- Dry Ice
- Insulated gloves
- Film canister
- Electric drill
- Shallow basin to hold water
- Rubber bands
- Sturdy cardboard or plywood

Safety Precautions: Use dry ice only with adult supervision. Never touch dry ice with your bare skin – it may cause frostbite! Use dry ice only outdoors or in a well-ventilated room to prevent buildup of carbon dioxide gas. Do not inhale vapors – inhalation of vapors may cause suffocation, since carbon dioxide displaces oxygen.

Procedure:
1. Drill a small hole in the lid of a film canister, about 4 mm in diameter.

2. Cut out a sturdy piece of cardboard or plywood in the shape of a boat, to whatever size you desire. Use rubber bands to attach the film canister to the boat.
3. Fill the film canister about halfway with water, drop in a piece of dry ice, and then quickly secure the lid.
4. Place in the basin of water and watch what happens. You may need to adjust the film canister so that the boat floats in the water as flat as possible.

Explanation: The boat is propelled by the escaping vapor and water from the hole in the film canister. According to Newton's Third Law of Motion, for every action there is an equal and opposite reaction. As the vapor and water escape from the hole, a force is exerted in one direction. As a result, an equal but opposite force in the other direction propels the boat forward.

Experiment # 37:
CAN ANTIFREEZE BE MADE TO FREEZE?

Objective: To discover if dry ice is capable of freezing antifreeze.

Materials:
- Dry Ice
- Insulated gloves
- Transparent disposable plastic cup
- Antifreeze

Safety Precautions:
Antifreeze contains ethylene glycol and is very poisonous. Store out of reach of children and wash hands after using. Use dry ice only with adult supervision. Never touch dry ice with your bare skin – it may cause frostbite! Use dry ice only outdoors or in a well-ventilated room to prevent buildup of carbon dioxide gas. Do not inhale vapors – inhalation of vapors may cause suffocation, since carbon dioxide displaces oxygen.

Procedure:
1. Pour about 50 mL of antifreeze into a plastic cup.
2. Add several pieces of dry ice to the

antifreeze. Observe carefully for several minutes. Is dry ice capable of freezing "antifreeze?"

Explanation: If you read the label of the antifreeze container, you can determine at what temperature it will prevent the radiator of your automobile from freezing. Since dry ice exists at temperatures below -78.5°C (-108.3°F), even the most hearty antifreeze will not provide protection at these temperatures. Don't worry, you are not likely to experience temperatures cold enough to freeze antifreeze even though such temperatures have been recorded on earth. The coldest temperature ever recorded on Earth was -88°C (-127°F) in Vostok, Antarctica on August 24, 1960. At temperatures that low, carbon dioxide in the air would actually turn into dry ice!

Experiment # 38:
CAN YOU COLOR DRY ICE?

Objective: To discover if food coloring will "stick" to dry ice.

Materials:
- Dry Ice
- Insulated gloves
- Plastic cups
- Ice cube
- Food coloring

Safety Precautions: Use dry ice only with adult supervision. Never touch dry ice with your bare skin – it may cause frostbite! Use dry ice only outdoors or in a well-ventilated room to prevent buildup of carbon dioxide gas. Do not inhale vapors – inhalation of vapors may cause suffocation, since carbon dioxide displaces oxygen.

Procedure:
1. Place a regular ice cube in a plastic cup and a chunk of dry ice in another cup. Place a few drops of food coloring directly on the ice cube. Observe.
2. Now repeat with the dry ice. What do you

observe? Can you find any liquids that will adhere to dry ice?

Explanation: Water is a polar substance, meaning it is composed of molecules having both positive and negative ends. As a result, water is termed the universal solvent. Its very strong polarity enables it to dissolve a wide variety of substances.

But not everything will dissolve in water. A nonpolar substance (such as oil) will not dissolve in water, but a polar substance (such as food coloring) will. This leads to the principle that "like dissolves like." At room temperature, the ice cube will have a fine layer of water on its surface due to melting, which will enable the food coloring to dissolve. As a result, the food coloring will color the ice cube.

The dry ice, on the other hand, has no layer of liquid on its surface, since it undergoes sublimation. Even if you had a layer of liquid CO_2 on its surface (which is possible at high pressures) the food coloring still would not dissolve, since CO_2 is a nonpolar substance. So no matter how hard you try, you cannot color dry ice. Not even oil or paint will stick to dry ice.

Another reason for this phenomenon is that a piece of dry ice at room temperature is constantly sublimating. There will always be a layer of gas surrounding the piece of dry ice, making it nearly impossible for anything to stick to it!

Experiment # 39:
QUICK THAW

Objective: To discover the effect of certain metals on the sublimation rate of dry ice.

Materials:

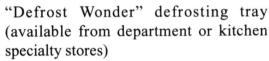

- Dry Ice
- Insulated gloves
- "Miracle Thaw" or "Defrost Wonder" defrosting tray (available from department or kitchen specialty stores)

Safety Precautions: Use dry ice only with adult supervision. Never touch dry ice with your bare skin – it may cause frostbite! Use dry ice only outdoors or in a well-ventilated room to prevent buildup of carbon dioxide gas. Do not inhale vapors – inhalation of vapors may cause suffocation, since carbon dioxide displaces oxygen.

Procedure:

1. Place a piece of dry ice on top of your defrosting tray. If a defrosting tray is not available, simply paint a cheap aluminum pan black, which will serve the same purpose.

2. At the same time, place a piece of dry ice on the counter to serve as a control. Which piece of dry ice sublimates faster?

Explanation: The commercially available defrosting trays do indeed work very well, enabling frozen food to be thawed very quickly. They work so well it seems like magic. But it is actually chemistry at work. The secret of the defrosting tray is that it is made of aluminum. Aluminum has a fairly high heat capacity and also an excellent rate of thermal conductivity. A high heat capacity means that it contains a fairly large amount of energy, which it releases as it cools. The high rate of thermal conductivity means that it releases its energy very quickly, thus enabling foods to thaw rapidly. The fact that it is painted black also helps, since black objects are able to absorb, and thus release, more energy than lighter colored objects.

When the piece of dry ice is placed on the defrosting tray, the aluminum quickly cools, releasing its energy in the form of heat, causing rapid sublimation. This explains why metals feel so cold to the touch when it is cold outdoors.

NOTES:

_____

_____

_____

_____

_____

_____

_____

_____

_____

_____

_____

_____

_____

39 Dazzling Experiments with Dry Ice

NOTES:_____

_____

_____

_____

_____

_____

_____

_____

_____

_____

_____

_____

_____